CHASE SOMETHING WORTH THE KILL

(REDOX)

POEMS OF LOVE, DEATH, AND RESURRECTION

BY RYAN MORROW

I asked him once, "Do you believe in resurrection?"
In-between sips of cheap whisky, he calmly replied "Everyday"

"Only after disaster can we be resurrected. It's only after you've lost everything that you're free to do anything. Nothing is static, everything is evolving, everything is falling apart"
- **Chuck Palahniuk**

"The call of death is a call of love. Death can be sweet if we answer it in the affirmative, if we accept it as one of the great eternal forms of life and transformation."
- **Hermann Hesse**

"Writer's block results from too much *head*. Sever your head. Pegasus and thus poetry, were born from Medusa when her head was cut off. You must be reckless when writing. Be as crazy as your consciousness allows."
- **Joseph Campbell**

What is ultimately meaningful in one's life? What goals should we set. Who should we become? What is worth protecting? What should we sever and what should we leave behind? How much is too much, how much is not enough? When does it get easier or less complicated? Who can we truly trust? Is progress even real? Where is the line between confidence and arrogance? Compassion and neglect. Love and obsession. Grief and oblivion. Sloth and meditation. Exploration and colonialism. There are those in this world who will tell you their path is the path to a better life, but who's life? And is it even possible to follow another's course? Or does the bridge dissolve just as soon as it is crossed? There's an old saying, "the only difference between a drug dealer and a pharmacist is who takes your money." I feel the same not just about chemical substances, but ideas as well. It is far too easy to adopt the thoughts, feelings, and experiences of others. Yet without the experience itself, filtered and processed through any individual it decays into ephemeral sand. Wish-cycling. The flotsam and jetsam of another's mind. A bleached simulacrum. An imitation. A faded copy.

The essential thread that weaves itself through the vast fabric of human experience is Quality. That elusive and yet certain element. That hard to pin down colossus. That blinding shadow of truth. An endless reflection in a pristine mirror that never changes, only amplifies, and confirms. Quality is all that matters and all that ever could matter. It is found and perhaps understood through a process of mental fire. A forging that requires hard and relentless attention. The product is never held in completion. It only exists in that honest and pure chrysalis of transformation. It is not so much the product at some proverbial end, but rather a mirage that is always becoming. Defining itself through necessity. Food for a forming god. Quality is the ultimate sustenance for Man's Soul. One must always, Chase Something Worth the Kill.

This book was written way back in 2015. It was my first stab at really expressing myself in a cohesive and perhaps exuberant way. It is deeply flawed and naive. Riddled with amateur musings and dances dangerously close to that repugnant thing called platitude. Yet in all this I believe it to still contain value. A poignant bookmark in time. It is a book about love and loathing, discovery and disappointment, the truth of death, and the immaculate cleansing of resurrection. It is only fitting that this book is itself a kind of resurrection. If you're out there E(Lie), this book is also the Universe's biggest middle finger. You are cosmic garbage.

Thank you for reading and experiencing.

with Love and Madness,

-Ryan Morrow

Credit to Robert M. Persig and "Zen & the Art of Motorcycle Maintenance.

LOVE IS DEATH DEATH IS LOVE

I can hear death's high heels
clicking down the spiral staircase
I can feel her coming so close
all the hairs on my neck stand alert

She is casual and cavalier
with her sex and her doom
She is like a razor that glides
across my thinning soul

I wear a mark upon my heart
I have an X carved into my skull
I am a wound that throbs
evermore profound as she nears

I bleed out everything
and then I bleed a little more

A cold wind blows
lifting her sleek black skirt
just enough for me
to catch a glimpse of the end

Before it all sinks down below
Before fate gathers at my feet
Before colors known and unknown
flood through my mind's eye

My passions are incredibly ripe
desperate to be consumed
Time itself is drunk
with her potent presence

I am but a fleeting moment
slipping through her slender fingers
A grain of sand in her pocket
of wandering dreams

Every time we come around this bend
it feels as though it might be the first

beginning, and yet ending
simultaneously together

I never wanted to live forever
I just didn't want this rapture to be wasted

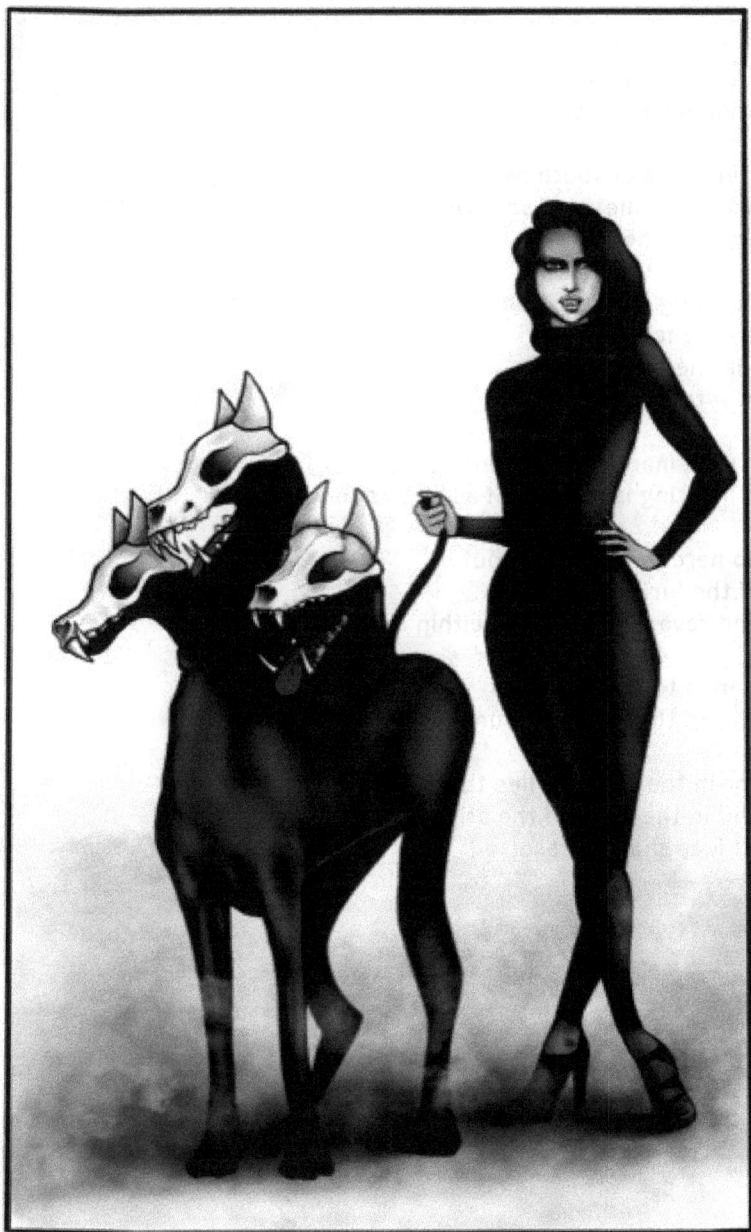

THE MASOKISS

Years of solitude
had left plaques
upon his tired bones

Memories of youth remain
like a silhouette of sorrow
upon his heart

Avoiding the question
of love for so long
that he truly forgot
how to answer

A wise man in his life once said,
"The sting is never half as bad as the fear, boy"

So here's to stepping out
of the lurking shadows
and revealing the man within

Here's to puckering up
to kiss the vipers of duality

For in their venom lies the cure
and in the wake of the sting
all fear shall be resolved

BLINK

"You have eyes like the insides of grapes," she said
describing my distant gaze
beneath the willow tree canopy

The pale stars
winking their secrets
in some cosmic Morse code
far above us

We discussed space and time
while we drank deep into
our wine glasses

Somehow, it's these simple
and frail moments
that seem to *matter* most

The memories that stick around
that shine and endure
that persist and resist
the fading

I sit here now
looking up at the same
blinking suns
drinking the same red wine

pondering the infinite sky
that still clutches
the same dark secret

VANISH

There is a maniac
in us all

it does not want
your money
or your logic

it wants chaos
by the fistfuls

it wants the freedom
of a dying star

it must burn
until it burns out

There is a fiend
cut loose within our mind

it seeks the bottom
of every bottle

it craves disorder
and constant erosion

it thrives off
turning us inside out

There is a vampire
hidden in us all

it must drain to survive
and when beauty cries out
that beast *smiles*

and then vanishes
just as sure as
the sun does rise

INSTRUMENTAL

I've never mastered
an instrument
but on any given day
I can play a moment
like a Stradivarius violin

I can make your bones
rattle and dance
keeping rhythm
with the bass drum
in our chest

I can conduct
these aching bodies
to move from the grave
to the living-room dance floor

I never learned the banjo or guitar
but I can strum your heartstrings
if you promise to sing along

MOON SONG

lover, lover
against the wall

you are my goddess -
the sexiest
of all

lover, lover
forever toward you I fall

its's not a
one night stand
if we never sleep at all

THE ACT

If only...
I could fuck
the muse
right out of this
machine

burn away the truth
like so many
discarded poems

power is in the absence
and it just grows
and grows

ubiquitous fountains
regurgitating ancient wisdom
like a godhead orgasm

"Death is the path to Awe!"
and I willingly drown
in its vast expanse

the legs of the universe
spread before us all
open like a physics book

for there is no fear
in this execution
no shame in
extinction

we have nothing to lose
and only paradise
to gain

AS DEDICATED AS A GUILLOTINE

I grip my lovers
like there's a noose
around my neck

pulling the begging rope
with everything I've got

I hold my lovers
like hand grenades
with the pin already pulled

To let go now
would be the death of us all

I strangle every night
so it can't love another

I swallow down
the hemlock and nightshade
hoping for the best

I French kiss every horror
in the whore house
just to tempt the fates

I'll tie you to the latest hex
and bless this eternal doom

we are all just slaves to sex
from seed to exhausted bloom

Hush my pretty pet
violence is the only solution
for *innocence*

I am as dedicated as a guillotine
giving head like a death-machine

I will honor this bloodlust
and fill every basket
with your smiling serenity

SEASONS

My lust is perennial
it has seasons

and in the summer's
fading zenith
it blooms in full

understanding its
terrible and certain fate

it seeks destruction
by the fires of your eyes

one last demonstration
to prove its might

The moon's glow
shall not be wasted

as precious as a desert oasis
and stronger than carbonized steel

I push my intent like a mule
through the trenches of catharsis

while all the city lights flicker out
behind an arching feminine spine

my mind writhes
but the pain is unimportant

for I am erudite
with this death cult night

there is no *master* here
only two equal *slaves*

EXPLORER

I push another finger
into her open mouth

one more than
she really enjoys

I pull on her
lop-sided ponytail

just a little harder
then she can stand

I want her to know
that after the climax

she's really the one
in control

THE BOXER

It was one hell of a fight!
a stunning combo strait into
a total knockout

but I'm not talking about sports
or even punches

It's that perfect string of words
the syllables that just float together
like a Beethoven symphony

with no chance to evade
or even seek an exit

striking with accuracy
and perfect precision

the opponents of mind
drunk with awe and curiosity

fall into the pit
of pure imagination

every night you didn't
throw in the towel
another scar
another story to tell

surrendering to the madness
is just another kind of victory

ANTI BODIES

We walked off
every cliffside

yet we never sank
below the razor's edge

We dared all our demons
to come out and play

they danced awhile
and then retired

We took every risk
imaginable

only to find out
we had already won

We *emptied* our hearts
like dying orchids

but the decay only
made our soil burst
and then bloom once more

Our arms coiled tight
around the deepest night

We were strung-out on love
and immune to every clock

RAPUNSLUT

Let down your jet-black hair
and I'll drag my way back
to your deathly stare

I'll force my body through
every jagged keyhole
for just a glimpse inside your
Pandora's Box

Unravel your serpent tongue
and allow me to martyr myself
burning in that perfect poison
just to prove my bones are yours

Worship till
there's nothing left
to worship

Beg until
all the other beggars
fade away

Release your raven hemlocks
and teach me how to suffer
like a chosen one

Your voice is a choir of
angels and nooses
they steal my every breath

My soul is frozen
trapped upon your whims
sing me a death-rattle
sing me home

WHAT'S YOUR TYPE?

Mine has a hum -
a gentle purr

a crackling taunt
and a constant hunger

it softly whispers
and then moans for hours

it is persistent
with inescapable demands

Mine has a hum
a curious purr

it needs me
and somehow loathes me

and when I need it most
it seems indifferent

yet it has changed me
completely

Mine has a hum
and purrs like a small
but dangerous cat

What's your Type
of
Writer?

WINE FROM GRAPES

They say it's never just one thing
but more times than not
when it really counts
it's one all-consuming thing

We know when we should bail
or when we shouldn't enter
yet we still do
time and time again
we eat the forbidden fruit
we dance upon the grave

we dive headfirst
into the shallow waters
we play with matches
surrounded by cans of gasoline

It just feels too damn good
when the chemicals are aligned
when the middle finger is held high
to emerge from Hell's depths
smiling and still intoxicated

There is a certain kind of life
that is forged by the kilns of survival
There is a prime reward granted
from the carcass of the beast
that you were forced to chase
by the love that held a knife to your throat
the *Kill* that that almost killed you

No TV dinner is worth dying for
but a meal for the heart just might be
it has such a delectable taste
rare and raw
with an indivisible nature
a thing of blood and beauty
when all other things have perished

When the many become just one
when all life beneath the sun disappears
only to return under the sacred moonlight
that's the thing to chase
that's the one you've been after all along
the prize and the purity of passion

It arises from emptiness
but shall fall into every-thingness
it precipitates from a brutal drought
it is scrapped from the bottom of it all

Everyone I know who has a story to tell
has fought to get it
almost died to own it

Allow
your
grapes
to
suffer

THE PUSHER

I'm writing because
my drink is telling me
I must

I'm writing this because
the night is vanishing
like all the rest

I'm writing -
but just barely
to honor the ones
that came before

I'm writing
with bad posture
and terrible grammar
yet a beautiful intent

I'm staining
this clean white page
to extol
the bleeding moment

calling out
to utter strangers
and ancient friends
to commune

I'm writing
to get nothing
for nothing
and in that nothingness
we are *free*

STARVING ARSONIST

This
is going
to hurt
I can
promise
you

but in
exchange
for all your
pain
you will receive
a world
of perspective

One where ashes
do not reassemble
but the flames
are guaranteed
to change
the mood

ROMAN ROMANCE

Love is a *War* -
so much skin
doused in battle sweat

craving the victory
of each other's hearts

ranks of men and women
just the dull /weapons of fate

trillions of unions
and always the same result

the night steals our corpses away
for tomorrow's harvest

Love is Hell -
just so many burning bodies
pleading for mercy

craving an exit
that will quench our minds

hordes of endless lovers
just a feast for fate

infinite chances
and always the same result

the fire takes our memories
and the embers - wait

OSCILLATIONS OF POWER

Tonight
I am Genghis Khan
conquering my fear
like a peasant village

Tonight
I become Julius Caesar
reinventing time
and kingdom alike

Tonight
I obey no rule, law, or code
my battle cries
shall reach the edges of the Earth

my heart beats fresh and new
with striking desire
my blood burns inside me
like magma in the world's center

I'm unable to stop
what has begun
the only way out
is through

Tonight
I am Neil Armstrong
tasting every moment
with a virgin moan

Tonight
I become Thich Quang Du'c
I am everything
but tomorrow I will be

nothing but ashes

RIND

Her eyes have a way
of peeling back the moment
exposing me like an autopsy

it's the *precision* in her gaze
cutting like a scalpel blade
it does not waver, nor can it lie

there's the brutal truth -
and then there's the creeping wisdom
that always follows

one I can live with -
the other will destroy
us all

~~ALL PRO~~ - NO CON

We are all slouching
through this life
slowly decaying
from innate diseases
while the cop cars
race wildly around corners
trying to *serve* us papers

meanwhile the bills
pile higher and higher
the list of "could 'a would 'a should-haves"
grows ever longer
while the earth is torn to dust
by the shaking hands of chaos

we are just useless meat
surrounded by the hungry jackals
of the American Nightmare

with all this -
I still don't ask for much
a god damn spot in the sun
an occasional bottle of gin
and a beautiful round ass
within reach

fuck
all
the
rest

DECLASSIFIED

You will know it when...
the present *now* becomes your supreme leader
all vessels sailing to its command
all flesh seduced into surrender

When you cannot see a thing
and yet you *know*
beautiful and dangerous
its wings of fire spread before you
It wants you to want it
and you want it in full

You shall thirst for its resonance
for it stabilizes galaxies
its energy increases your own

you can feel it penetrate the densest of moments
you crave the feast made union in its words
merging into in a blooming dialect

It will become your sustenance
tethering cell to sinew
without it you wither and wilt

It un-hollows you with saccharine depth
and waters your soul until it nearly bursts
you close your two eyes and open another

a skeleton key - that unlocks all doors
a universal tool - that remakes all things

You will know it when...
everything is mutual and symbiotic
It pulls as you push, pushes when you pull
spinning, vibrating, and pulsing
in harmony with spacetime
an original score to a very old story

BREAK THE FEVER

Crawl upon me
hungry creature
consume and satisfy
your every need

Drink deep
and pay no mind
to the rising sun

I am now
consumable
eat your fill

I promise you
we are impervious
to the outside world

Don't you dare stop
until the itch has fled
and sunk below

If we never fear
the consequences
then we can have no masters

WHAT I AM

I am what I have devoured
and the scraps I leave behind

I am what I destroy
and the wreckage in the wake

I am a war
of bodies and lovers
both its casualties
and victories

I am a nightmare
an endless dream *awaked*

I am an open wound
that does not desire to heal

I am an idea
ever-growing untamed
without a home
nor destination

I am multitudinous questions
without a single answer
a jigsaw puzzle with only
mangled pieces

I am the universe
inhabited by one -
a man trapped
within the dungeon of self

I am the universe
seeking to know itself -
a beast inside a dungeon
no longer able to contain itself

DEEP SPACES

Quasar woman
with your pulsing beauty
you integrate my every desire

I'm drawn against
all will power

your sexuality
is its own kind of gravity
a body like a blackhole

few have dared to enter
and none escape that do

Supernova woman
your body is a cosmic mystery
yet it resonates into my inner core

I'm curious against
all logic and reason

eyes like two dying stars
all knowing and *improbable*

nothing could compare
and nothing ever shall

IMMACULATE INCEPTION

There is something innately profound
about the vast
and empty landscape
of a fresh page

A screaming, yearning desert
begging to be explored
and trampled
by desperate love

To be marked and imprinted
calling out from distant unknowns
pleading to make contact -
to be *understood*

From a dimension all together alien
comes a fluidic voice
a foreign speaker that dares
to name the faceless hollow

The mysterious forces
of ink and pigment bind
the ceremony to its master
unaware of its lasting impressions

Coming often with vitality and courage
at others fear and apprehension
the cascading results nearly endless
yet the sacrifice always the same

Upon the blank lifeless alter
of parchment
a ritual is executed
an offering of vulnerability

Spent and exhausted
the void gives birth
to a symbiotic entity
of past and present

Words are pure power
transforming and mutating
nothingness into somethingness
an alchemy of the highest order

PLATO IN MY MOUTH

It's dark
in my cave
darling
but it's also
quite warm

There's only
one way in
and no way out

My idea
of a better life
comes only
at the price
of more pain

Lonely is
the *ape*
who sold
his last great idea
to his zookeeper

Broken lay
the bones
of every warrior
by right and might

In my world
the beggars
die wise and
the rich men
starve

DISENCHANTED

There is no love left in that heart
only something imitating
pretending

a chameleon, a shade
a kind of shrewd predator
that kills what it cannot understand

There is a crazed barbarian
storming my castle gates
I recognize its danger
and that familiar perfume of death

Beware all temptresses!
you shall starve
on your knees
howling and begging
to enter

Yield all sorceresses!
call back your plastic gods
that give you false hope
and cheap glamor
you have failed

I will survive this
inside my fortress of reveries
crossing tongues with
the beautiful creatures
of an unsoiled imagination

TRIGGER FINGER

keep your finger
on that trigger
and keep me satisfied

keep pulling
on that trigger
and I'll never get depressed

keep shooting every excuse
we have to say no
strait through the fucking head

Bang Bang
bliss bliss
Bang Bang
you never miss

empty your (c)lips upon my heart
like an automatic pistol
I swear I won't complain
when you stop to reload

~~ADVANCED~~

While
you
were
busy
flirting
with
disaster

I
was
banging
death
against the
grandfather-clock

While
you
were
tempting
the
fates

I
was
already
feeding
the hundred
children
of my
doom

GORGON EYES

Ever since
the day I met you
I've been falling
like a row of dominos

just a cascade
tumbling down
destined to drown

Ever since
the day I saw you
I've never been able
to look away

just another victim
forever *stone*
forever alone

COSMIC ORGASMIC

They say "Psychedelic intoxication is a cheap escape"
some fabricated enlightenment or button of bliss
but we're too far armored for their salvo of useless arrows

They say something like, "What about your future?"
We respond, "Fuck *your* future -
it means nothing without the penetration of these moments"

They rattle on "But aren't you scared of the consequences?"
We scream "There is far greater consequence in your abstinence!
We fear nothing now - the universe blooms within us!"

If you open-up your mind
the cosmos will open her legs
and in-between those milky sways
pulsars and gravity waves
is *the* answer to the unasked question
a period at the end of a circular sentence

Our lives are like wet dreams
dripping with infinities
foreplay and heavy petting
in a much larger *score*
a sustained note in the celestial symphony

We are the fuel of consciousness
electro-chemical gods and goddesses
getting ever higher on imagination
synthesizing our bodies with our minds
through a molecular symbiotic divine

They say, "But that cannot be?"
We simply laugh and disappear

MIDDLE FINGER

Today is as good a day
as any ever will be

to shut off
the *damned* screens
to sever the head
of every politician

no racket
no diversion
cut the cords
of discontent

and crawl up
from the
cultural quicksand

drink deep
and smile hard

maybe even
try to laugh
hysterically

skip down the street
saying "FUCK YOU!"
to no one in particular

Today is as good a day
as any ever was

to just let go

SURGEONS OF FIRE

And so it begins again -
like so many times before
the smiles
the kisses
the pre-game jitters

We're going mad
losing ourselves to the beat
of our own chaos

we become rulers of
our own misfortune -
the molders of *human* clay

we are the surgeons of fire
burning the truth out slowly
as we hack chemical pleasures
from our soft brains

we parade around our skulls
making it rain serotonin and dopamine
we are the Native Post-Americans
dancing ourselves apocalyptic

we are downright cannibals
the cannibal elite!
feeding upon each other's creations
until tomorrow brings us
new flesh

THE BIG SUCK

I said yes.
and now
my gate is *open* wide
the vampires
come and go
as they please

I said yes.
and now
all my spells are cast
sucking me of power
and defenses

She drained it all
until a drop before dry
just enough
to allow my sorrow to return
just enough
for the pain to replenish

I said yes.
and now
I can never say no

SCRAPS & THANGS

Survival
has always

brought out
the best
in us

the beast
in us

now let us feast
on the very corpse
of *us*

so we can
truly thrive

WAX & HONEY

These memories are like spilled honey
every moment still sticky with her taste
once glorious and saccharine treats
now just cavities and stained sheets

These memories are but melted wax
that have infiltrated the tiniest parts of me
covering my fingertips like armored skin
unable to feel anything *new* to my chagrin

These memories are as a spent candle
that has burnt-out slow and complete
dripping down into my every pore
my heart has dissolved –
yet my mind still begs for more

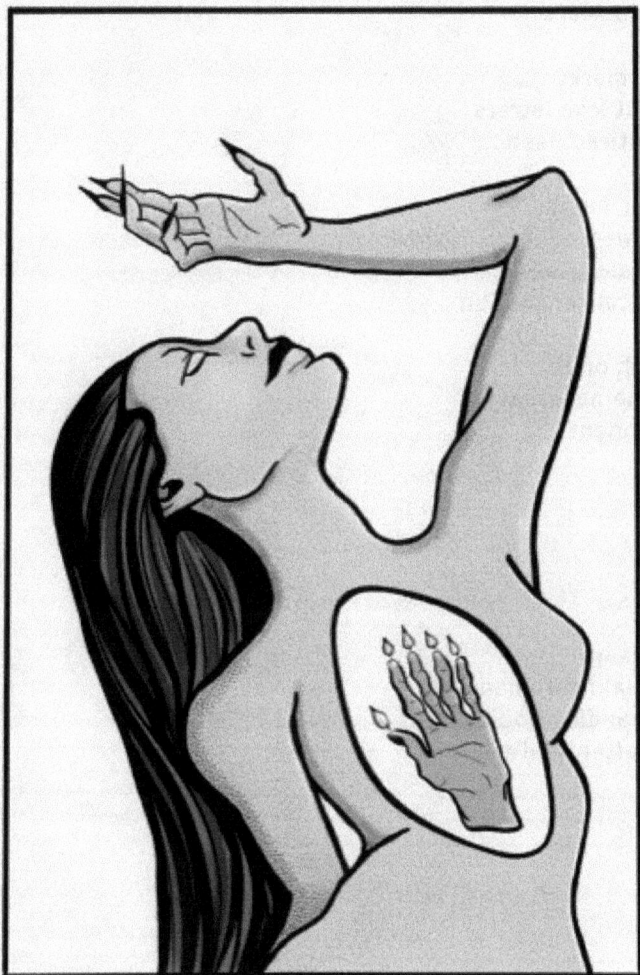

WITCH

your violence
hides in soft kisses
casual bruises
and old scars

these marks
are but love letters
to my tired flesh

in your blood
is brewed
some elevated
chemical concoction

in each of us
is some necessary
component

heart
brain
blood
bone

your fangs
are dual necromancers
commanding bodies
even after death

SALVAGED

My life had been discarded
into some proverbial junkyard
of solitude and sorrow

Cerberus the three-headed hound
stood guard at the rusty gates
of my haunted heart

but Alas you arrived!
in blazing light and fanged intent

my sweet heroine
my sacred heroin

your angelic perfume
pushing back the brimstone

your body the mythic battle-axe of old'
severing every head of the devil dog

your lips have nothing to offer
save the death of all my beasts

you have unearthed a great treasure
in the wasteland of me

you shave *salvaged* this man's love
from a growing despair

you are the fountain oasis
in my deepest of hells

HANDS OF THE WRITER

Write me a story
writer man

weave me a tale
made of golden words
take me
far far away

make me believe
that anything
is possible
that it was all worth
the struggle

Write something beautiful
ink mage

build me a castle
made from the bricks
of your mind
take me higher
and then higher still

make me forget
that any of this was ever real
that it was all just a silly dream
wrapped in yet another dream

Write me into a new world
word god

create me then uncreate me
destroy me in your image

Writer man
with your writer's hands
write me *softly*
away

LITERATURE

I have a growing suspicion
that I may not be
your end-all-be-all

that I am not your great war
nor your lasting *peace*

I'm beginning to think
I am neither your Greek tragedy
nor pure comic relief

I will not be your masterpiece
your Magnum Opus
nor your fatal release

I am but a catchy story
you like to read ever on repeat

MEDUSA OBLONGATA

Wherever you appear
my eyes are commanded
to follow

wherever you arrive
so shall the remains
of my soul

your beauty is a weapon -
a monster and
a goddess alike

no one escapes
without losing something
and gaining everything

we are victims
and we are artifacts
monuments to your power

we are but stone
and when you stare upon us
we are polished *perfection*

LABYRINTHIAN CREATURES

This life has been a fire of discovery
each new experience more vivid than the last
traveling through time and space with fluidity
love death and resurrection in perfect lucidity

navigating the immeasurable landscapes of mind
pioneering across chasms and crags of every kind
an alchemy of consciousness in each breath taken
hoping in some way that we might be awakened

We are such Labyrinthian creatures
wandering without aim
and yet endlessly curious

imploding as we expand
consuming as we are consumed
we are Matryoshka Dolls
of Love and Madness

spiraling and spinning round
to an unknown frontier we are bound
a wealth of possibilities
is just as crushing as it is liberating

submerged in potential
drowning in options
every moment of life
contains its little grain of death

Something moving on
and something left behind
woven tightly round our hearts
is a relentless resurrection

CIRCULAR BREATHING

attraction
is the birth
of desire

satisfaction
is its death

you and me baby
we live & die
in every breath

FOOD CHAIN

her succulent lips hide and wait
like a patient spider
in a bedroom made of silk

I wander aimlessly
towards her center
inextricably drawn to that siren moan

I can hear a door slamming shut
as the thick air holds
my breath in place

the webs of seduction
cling to my face
moistening me for the kill

in-between panic and an erection
my pleasure is irrelevant
to her hunger

coiled within this moment
is the sustenance
of a perfect death

CHAMELEON

She was no woman -
she was a beautiful monster
in a little black dress

I was hardly a man -
more of a clever beggar
in a thrift store suit jacket

Over several years and many 'a tears
I continued to inform her that
"You can't steal love like you do attention"

and that wicked dance
could never truly temper
my heart of glass

lust will always burn away
like so much gasoline
only momentarily changing
the color of the flames

but love will always remain
crystalline and pure
lying still
beneath the ashes

BEDROOM WARFARE

Now that I've got you inside
I couldn't dare let you out

I allow the music to cast its ancient spell
as I hold on to your warm body
with all the bravery I can muster

I am charging into love's battle
my tongue the appointed commander

every kiss an atom bomb
upon the frontlines

every whisper another casualty
of our resistance

this battlefield will soon be blessed
with our sacred sweat
and cursed by a holy threat

I lead my heart straight into certain death
sacrificed upon the most beautiful
of castle gates

my armies willingly drown in her pious moat
the moon ascends as we both surrender
to the rising waters

THE GIVER

You cum in multiples
but I just keep working

you howl out strange names
while I forge ahead

your claws beg for release
my stamina defies logic

your body quakes and shatters
I am at war with Aphrodite herself

You can't take it anymore
but I can't stop *giving* it

HYDRA

My mind has run off
wildly into the hills
attempting to escape
your sniper eyes
that stare pleadingly
back into mine
wanting more

Your knees push
down the very earth
digging for a way
out of our skin
and into more sin

My brain is consumed
and flooded
with images of your form
infinite ways to bend
and prove we are immortal

Your screams are
as gasoline to an eager fire
that I refuse to contain

Each orgasm
but a single severed head
of the monstrous hydra

In the empty space
is no great victory
but rather two more
hungry mouths to feed

THE VARIETIES OF RELIGIOUS EXPERIMENTS

You are my
needy narcotic
sweet and a bit chaotic
you make every flavor
new and oh-so exotic

You are my
ample amphetamine
a demon queen
of which I cannot help
but spill my spleen

You are a
perfect poison in a glass
of which none shall pass
without a healthy dose
and a glance at that ass

You are my
holy hallucinogen
a psychic mutagen
one in which I shall return
time and time again

HOWL CYCLE

between sunsets
between sheets
I worshiped you
like it was the last
day on earth

as if the only way
to quell
these primal needs
was to make our bodies
scream

in empty apartments
in strangers' cars
in abandoned fields

oblivious
to the greater world

howling like mad wolves
louder and louder
to false moons

turning sex
into a kind violence
is this a lover's den
or crime scene?

instead of catharsis -
in place of release
is but something *shattering*
upon its climax

and the desperate ache of a union
incomplete

REBIRTH

each and every night
I bathe in primordial ooze
letting the mystery of what's to come
soak deep into my skin
while creation and destruction dance

each option - every moment
like terrible ocean waves
crash upon the shores of consciousness
and leave the corpses of myth behind
I too am *perfect* chaos

the head is a storm alive
raging out of control
a mad sky filled with lightning thoughts
as the moon reflects the fire of her eyes
building the realms of the endless

I intend to be annihilated
and then resurrected on the spot
self-actualized by this tempest of wonder
from the bubbling foam of the mind
comes Chimeras never before seen

DELAYED

when death tickles us
we laugh hysterically

when death throws its jabs
we grin through our teeth

when death desires us
we make death *wait*

we are such pleasure delayers
death knocks and knocks
but never gets it

SUBLIME REWARD

I have climbed to the top
of this tremendous tree
not because it was *easy*
but because it was incredibly difficult

and now I have the strangest of fruit
squeezed between my fingertips
overripe and dripping wisdom
into my palms

I howl into the night sky
with the full capacity of my lungs
inextricably intoxicated -
drunk off the future these seeds shall sow

I have ascended to the peak
of this magnificent mountain
not because it was required
but because it was demanded

and now I have an incredible view
seared deep into my memories
lush and blooming meaning
within my heart

I say nothing at all
overwhelmed by the virtue of bliss
a paradise earned
is one that can never be taken

BAPTIZED BY PAIN

I awaken once more
engulfed in flames

a thousand open wounds
without *closure*

I am blessed with survival –
and baptized by pain

serving my masters
by refusing to die

I am made of scars
a mosaic of failed attempts

a perpetual warrior
with endless monsters

I am cursed by survival -
healed only by death

an ancient text
palimpsest with gibberish

I am the resurrected man
forced to repeat his tragedies

every moment a gift
everyone after that a living hell

CHALK LINE

the world is just one big ghetto baby
and we are its orphan children
filled with madness

running wild down its dark alleyways
and playing Russian Roulette
with our sadness

we were raised by the sound of
click click click
and then tossed to the curb
like a cheap trick

we left fire in our footsteps
letting our laughter
carry us to the end of time

we held hands like lovers
drawing one big chalk-line
around our city of crime

we spun round a spiral
playing chutes then ladders
seduced and dared to enter

mesmerized by the rattle
we danced to our deaths
but never found the center

FANGS FOR BANGS

I feel like the monster
at every party
ready and willing
to gorge upon flesh
to indulge in every poison
to dare the fates themselves

I will feast until
there is famine
my eyes are nothing more
than gnashing teeth

I understand -
that everyone is starving
filled with a craving
but we are too civilized
and tamed by good manners

holding back the howl
extinguishing a flaring lust
enslaving an ancient request

but the beast has arrived
to fire the first shot
to set this night ablaze
Behold! The fangs of *desire*

it's going to be a
beautiful bloodbath
the kind you
never wash off

our hearts have demanded
a new apocalypse
the kind that
changes everything

LIBRARY

Scars are but bookmarks
saved upon our skin
so that we never forget
all the places that we've been

Some of us just can't decide
on where the best parts lie
or where the story truly began

LIVE AND DIE BY THE PEN

There is a violence in the written word
a displacing force
a neuronal revolution
a death and a rebirth
of stale ideas into something new

There is a warrior seated in the mind of every poet
ready to annihilate the world they know
or be annihilated by it
a transformation of flesh into meaning
by purging their every thought

There is sacred tree that hides in the literary heart
bearing endless fruits that drip with poison nectar
to eat is to understand
and yet be consumed
waiting in your death rattle is the prize

There is a silence between every raindrop
too quick to remember
and yet it is there we pine to capture
the vacancy in the void
the absence of everything

In perfect peace
blooms the great war
grab your *weapon* of choice

CRONUS

Alpha
sun
is rising

Omega
moon
soon to follow

We breathe in
everything
just to exhale
it all

We keep
nothing -
such is the way
of it all

Alpha
sun
has risen

Omega
moon
falls forever

Father Time
is ever *famished*
and he shall
devour all
his children

A NAME IN STARLIGHT

I've spread myself
so paper thin across this town
that I've begun to snap apart
and coagulate anew

like a spiral galaxy
some parts are ever burning
brilliant and hot
with vitality and hope

while others
have died long ago
desolate and cold
waiting for nothing

there is a common thread
stitched amongst it all
a hidden cosmic web
that vibrates and hums

always with her name

NICHE

Let's just say -
I'm a niche market

the potential stranger
around every corner

a rare vintage
for a special occasion

an eclectic collector
with specific tastes

the afterhours
sideshow attraction

a rarity in the back room
of an abandoned shop

Let's just say -
I'm the kind of weird

you're not sure if
you want to get *weird* with

GREATER CHAOS

Toss another
revelation
into the blazing fire

watch as they smolder
hot and strange

just new elements
for the universe
to abuse

throw all your
epiphanies
upon the funeral pyre

observe them dissolve
into the greater chaos

Man in all his wisdom
has been eclipsed
by his own trick

just perpetual amnesia
a prisoner
doomed to *forget*

RADIOACTIVE

shimmering with danger
no longer a stranger
to your ghastly glow

wet like a nightmare
locked in a death stare
I'm *dying* just to know

drawn to neon seduction
headed for certain destruction
a prisoner to your lightshow

KNOWLEDGE IS PAIN

Stacks of books keep piling higher and higher upon the shelves
all the words fucking and fusing
mutating and transforming in my mind
reaching like desperate beggars toward the flickering lightbulbs

So many days, years, centuries, eons of ideas
heaps of memories, stories, lifetimes, the plotlines of humanity
endless pain, joy, love, insanity yet to be resolved

There is the subterranean, terrestrial, intergalactic, astral
historical, imaginary, surreal, hypothetical
the blurred lines of fact, fiction, delusion, and terra incognito

I'm on fire and thriving in the paradise of language
I'm frozen and paralyzed in the hellscape of language
There is a rapture and yet an oblivion between the lines

The soul like a lost ship is caught
in the maelstrom of man's *knowledge*
all of mankind's sad attempts at understanding

What does it all add up to? Where do we fit in?
Do you feel solace, peace, purpose or escape?
Are we hopeless, limitless, bound or free?

Can we be satisfied or merely pacified?
Is there meaning or only momentary survival?
Can it all be sustained or is it doomed to black rain?

Is it just a formula yet to be solved? Or data computed?
A puzzle yet to be assembled.
Is there a poetic salvation or only scientific solutions?

The books continue to pile ever higher on the shelves
on the floor, on every remaining surface
The words are growing wild, untamable, unpronounceable
reaching for the great omnipotent castle in the sky

NEW FACE

Evil is but a mask
pulled from an ancient gallery
and when we wear its twisted face
we are under its spell

our hands capable
of unimaginable efforts
tempting the beast
to come out and play
to abandon their cavern
and spread its wings
like cosmic fire

to swallow the world whole
or consume it piecemeal
either way it disappears

Alas, there is mercy
for us sinners
as we bear witness
to yet another
beautiful sunrise
of we which we rarely deserve

Basking in the full light
we relish in yet another
opportunity to destroy

BAD WIZARD

I'm not searching for the *next* line
just to impress you
some vapid string of sentences
to sell a book or gain fame

I want what's behind the velvet curtain
I want the wizard hung!
I need the sick sad truth brought to justice
on a guillotine stage

I don't want you the reader –
to care or feel anything in particular
I want to strangle you with inspiration
for you to rediscover parts of yourself
you thought had gone extinct

I don't want your instant satisfaction
or some sycophant's praise
I want the utter ruin of a daring astronaut
that pushed beyond their limit

I don't want your damned comparisons
I want all memories destroyed
tabla rasa of the mind
to experience something out of nothing

HOLLOW AND HOWLING

The sex was never enough
pulling on fistfuls of raven black hair
digging nails deep into porcelain skin
and always still
the howling void

The lust was never enough
making the creature howl out to new gods
spread vulture - every scrap was mine
and yet still
the hollow morning

I had endless opportunities
to master your queendom of sorrow
where the spoils of a thousand
bedroom wars were laid bare
but it was still not enough

I was not enough
but I gave you and your *hell*
all of my fire

EXTRACTION

There is a skill in
extracting *quality*
from deep intoxication

Without crossing
the gates of oblivion

There is an odyssey to be had
monsters to be slain
and lovers to be worshiped

Manifestos to be written
rewritten and then burned

I shall become your pagan creature
stalking the pages of your holy maze

I intend to set endless fires in your mind
carve my name into the heart of it all

We were told not to eat of the forbidden apple
and so we cut the damn tree down

We made books from its accursed core
and brewed cider from the blood of its fruit

Drunk and defiant we plant our seeds
and wait as the flowers of evil bloom

ESCAPE THE DREAM

The clouds above the skyline
glitch in haunting colors
neon messages flicker their broken promises

a low siren moans from somewhere in the distance
everyone looks lost and helpless
as if they just escaped the zoo

what is this ache that demands such attention?
drawn like an iron magnet
to pheromones and wet heat

we need so little
yet we lust for so much
feeding an ever-open mouth
with new poisons

our dreams manifest into twisted realities
we are mutants crawling toward desperate salvations
leaving a glowing trails of regret and sorrow

lost in crooked streets of our own design
ever deeper in and
ever deeper down

in the eyes of every stranger
is the *truth* of it all -
love is but one step away
from madness

MIDNIGHT MUSIC

Your lust is a record
and I play it on repeat

each groove in the vinyl
becomes a welcome trench
of which I cannot escape

Your love is a record
that I can't stop spinning

the needle piercing
through the plastic
and my soul the same

Your body is pure fidelity
and my heart is perfectly tuned

GAME OF THRONES

All excuses
wither
and the fear
is destroyed

All doubt
vanishes
the rage
made weak

I am but a servant
to the will of lust

Her lips drip wet
with power and
forgiveness

Her legs unfurl
a world of pleasure
awaits

She invites me
to her throne room
and I proudly sacrifice

all my days
to the glory
of the queen

STRANGE SYNCHRONICITY

I found it
in the strangest of places
I found it
when I least expected to
I found it
when I thought it could no longer
be found

I found it
between the cracks
of perception

I found it
dancing alone
and in darkness

Out of rhythm
but perfectly in-sync
to some hidden clock

It plays by its own rules
free and unnamed

It had its own scales
weightless and unmeasured

Never expect to receive
what you don't deserve

Always praise the love
of a complete stranger

REVERSE PSYCHOLOGY

Do not fret my darling
in the deepest and darkest
of our desperation
lies our greatest chance
to repair

Our fears shall
find themselves
hollowed out -
with nothing
more to gain

Our wits shall be
sharpened
by these trials
polished
by our pain

Wisdom will
blossom
like a royal iris
from the thick
winter ice

HERO WITHOUT A FACE

A concept geneticist
mad linguistic scientist

twisting and mangling
changing and mutilating
all these chimeras of the mind

everything and anything becomes possible
there is a multi-verse within our heads

dreams are just the seeds for new realities
imagination a way to absolve our dualities

We chip away at the mountain of mystery
and mold our images into the stone

We make the creature walk!
pouring our pain into its veins

We make the creature waltz!
injecting our ache into its heart

sculpt a masterpiece
by removing
the *excess*

let the words rage like a river
from the extinction
of each moment

WHITE FLAG

I could write a thousand poems
that might impress you
but I'm only after one

The one that makes the ship of your heart
skip, stutter, and then crash
into the craggy rocks

Paradox is my god
made of ink and syllable
stalking between these pages

We cast our best words into
the ocean's vast body
and watch the waters ripple
and then fall silent

Contradiction is the only cure
for all our desperation
and helpless quest for absolution

We toss our greatest poems into
the world's raging fire
and watch as the flames roar
and then laugh

Only when we surrender
to the chaos
will that same chaos
finally take us home

GRUESOME GORGEOUS

Annihilation Tongues
lick the smoking tops
of our apocalypse guns

Gruesome and yet Gorgeous
a horror habitat of
Mad Max machines

pulsing
grinding
and screaming our names

blood points
headshots
and super kills

Slasher sex in the
dead of night

poison pussy
chaos cock
perfect penetration

eat out the core
regurgitate
repeat

CHECK AND MATING

Black Knight
to Queen's bedside C4
your move *Death*

A power piece is taken
but the game isn't over yet

Laughing
I suggest
a different game

Possibly Poker
or Russian Roulette?
(She does have the face for it)

Maybe Dice
or Spin-the-Bottle?

Your move Death

ALBATROSS

Mayday Mayday
I'm going down
and absurdly fast

My sanity has jumped ship
along with these useless crates
of serotonin

There is an uncontrolled fire
in the captain's quarters
without an exit

While the sun burns bright above
taunting a future that
will never come

I hold on with iron fist
to this last bit of sweet
intoxication

It will serve its purpose
to the *bitter* end

I scream out song and verse
to the passing albatross

if only to remind myself of
the beauty in our certain doom

COCOONED

She impresses me
without even trying

She heals every wound
that I have yet to receive

Her body is a silk cocoon
where I am nurtured and safe

Her touch holds pure sunlight
and I glow in the darkest night

There is a balance in our kiss
adding and subtracting
like waves upon the shore

We both walk effortlessly
onto the water's surface

believing it to be possible
and so it becomes

LOOSE CHANGE

When the kiss
no longer
lights the fire

When the lay
can no longer
calm the beast

When the edge
of every blade
is dull and tired

the eyes sink
and the heart is
abandoned

you damn right
I'll spend the extra $5.49
on the good stuff

SUPERCONSCIOUS

I need to stop getting exactly what I want
exactly when I want it
It's bad for my ego
bad for the art
bad for business
and business was good
when I was a bit broker
a bit more run-down
out of luck
out of time
out of woman

When I was in desperate need
when something wasn't quite right
that's when the muse
kicked down the door

A broken heart gives you so much to write about
to rage and pout about
a reason to spell your name
in neon blood across the city streets
to spill your guts
to the cosmic vacuum of time and space

Tonight I think I'll get tough
and toss my typewriter through the window
tonight I think I'll drink one too many
headbutt my television and
take a shit on my expensive bed sheets

The trick is to not get too comfortable
to self-destruct right before the zenith
to humble yourself through attrition

Tonight I will become my own worst enemy
and before the sun comes up I will have something
valuable to write about
Damn - here comes that bastard now...

PRESSURE

Love becomes meaningless
when all you can remember
are the kill scenes

just two dead bodies
in a twin bed like some
long-forgotten cemetery

put enough pressure
on a flawless diamond
it's still just a handful

of glitter and *dust*

SHE GUEVARA

She was a rebel
gliding between options
like a black cat down dark alleys

she never begged
cause she never had to

It all fell to her feet
simple toys in her game
just devotees to her mass appeal

She was a rebel
and she wanted me to go to war

She was charmed by my destruction
watching as I danced and writhed
a man in flames

She had supple steady hands
slowly extracting out the romance
like a surgeon or a *butcher* from my chest

I was a wet seed engorged with love
and nowhere to be planted
She taunted me with endless soil

Overwhelmed I became rabid
a twisted and feral creature
She remained the steadfast rebel

desperate to champion my paramour
I became the berserker
battling my soul into human dust
nothing left to burn

She was a rebel
and she demanded
my heart on a stick

FALLEN FROM GRACE

Where are you hiding?

I can sense your power
and mass effect
I can feel the pull
of your gravity
and the heat of love's engine

but I see no crumbs to follow
not a trace
nor a clue

only lights flashing
images pulsing
everything ephemeral
transient
untethered

I catch only glimpses
of shifting beauty
and glitches
of extreme horror

I am lost
understanding
nothing

My passion is now
like a fallen emperor
who can no longer feed
the peasants of his heart

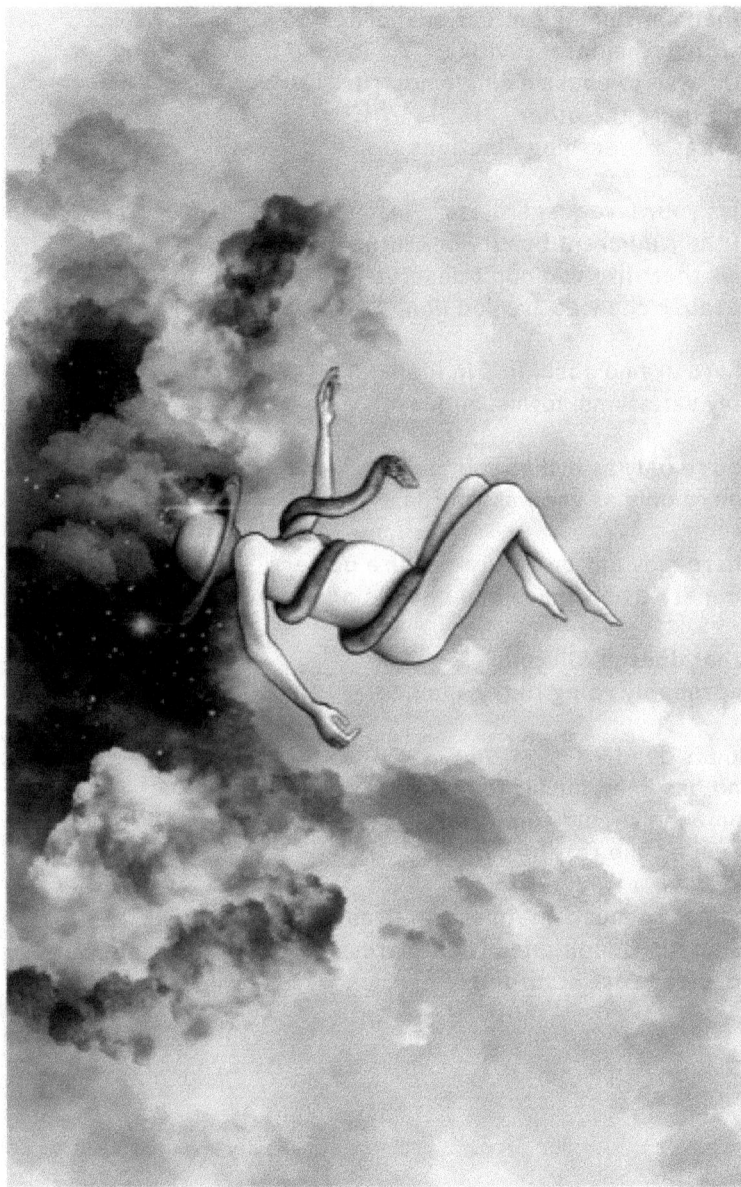

BATTLE AXE 10M

When consuming recreational drugs
through the nasal cavities
it is wise to abuse a single nostril
and spare the other
for basic breathing functions

Kiss your lover regardless
of their inherent beauty or status
kiss them like you don't deserve it
because chances are you don't

There are no absolutes in life
only variations, forms, and levels

You're only as evil as you feel
you're only as good as your last kiss

There may not be a purpose or a pattern
no matter how much one desires one to exist

What doesn't kill you
is probably going to try again

God is dead
and has been for far too long
someone should come and
clean up the rotting carcass

It's not so much an American Dream
as an Air-Conditioned Nightmare
So, please act accordingly

A WELL DRESSED DEAD MAN

I am a dead man
in wolves' clothing

I devour the night
so I may live again
tomorrow

these scars are relics
from all my
forgotten memories

I am a dead man
in a three-piece suit

walking through life
like the flames of hell

my eyes are an archive
holding equal parts
pain, love, & madness

I am a dead man
but you still have life to give

INTOXICATED ENDLESS

I am one
and yet I am many

I am ancient
and I am new all the same

I beg the darkness
to give me a name

My lust is chimerical
kissing me like
1,000 hungry snakes

I stare into the void
waiting for new lovers
to appear

I swallow fire
and teethe on
a black widow's spine

I'm intoxicated endlessly
on strange exiles
from beyond

All my masters lie
dead at my feet
emptied of their power

I make art from their bones
sculptures from their hollow hearts

I sell chaos on the street
in exchange for a buzz

I'll breakdown this death-machine
for the price of a laugh

NIGHT TERROR

I have awoken once again
trapped in a twilight frenzy -
my mind like a swarm
of stinging bees

my body a semi-conscious anchor
dragging along the ocean floor

I find myself un-dressed
and vulnerable
like a serpent of myth
my new flesh wet with chaos
and opportunity

Previous cycles
have mangled every key
and broken the lock
to my escape

I am forced by silent laughter
to accept this looping tragedy

to eat the rotten fruit
and drink the poisoned wine

Time stretches and
then folds upon itself
I remain lost and untethered
in a none-waking nightmare

spinning up and then
spinning down
in perpetual spiral

I must continue this process
until my dread finally
transforms itself
into bittersweet sleep

DIRTY TALK

She screamed
and pleaded
for him to,
"Fuck my brains out!"

evading
the obvious
problem

he fucked
his own
sanity away
instead

CRUCI BROKEN

All our futures cloaked in night
so I burn every crucifix I can ignite
just to keep us in the burning light

If death was not the end
and nature not our friend
we can stop our efforts to pretend

All our sacred gardens rotting
fruit upon the vine is sobbing
defiant hearts that won't stop throbbing

If death is not the end
perpetual cycle we must contend
no sleep nor salvation to defend

All our faith buried in the tomb
scent is wafting - death perfume
we pray to the *dirt* –
that something better might bloom

If death is truly not an end
it's all too much to comprehend
the fallacy of man to transcend

SLOW TEETH

Turn-ons:

the sound of your voice
whispering
"There is no escape"

your eyes
when you realize
this is all
we have left

your legs like
slow teeth
fused in a
famished beast

grinding me to dust

Turn-offs:

knowing that
when the day breaks
neither of us
will care

NIGHTMARE THRONE

Allow this possession to move all your objections aside
allow these spirits to drink the weight of themselves

I seek all the comforts of a *nightmare* throne
self-destruction is my battle-axe to the bottom

I slang heartbreak to the minotaur on the grass-corner
we're all just trying to buy our ticket out of the maze

Bang Bang goes my brain on the LARGE FONT
as I keep pace with the diehards and desperate immortals

the universe may be infinitely vast
but our finite night is running low on white lines

What I wouldn't do to die in the grip
of a poet's fever dream - drowned in love and black ink

Be not the tourist that cheapens all experience
but the native who is synonymous with the land

eat the dirt like medicine
bathe in the Earth's magma core

Shaman of the cosmos
guide me to your spiritual cheesecake
O' Wolf god! O' Wolf god!
let me dissolve into to your saliva nectar

I deny the cheap enlightenment
I defy the lowest fruit
I dare to never forget

for there is a masked truth pulsing
through a veil ever thinning

I want the deep and obscured
I want the taboo and sacred
unmolested by man
unadulterated by exposure

Are you willing to
work work work for it?
to die for it?
keep dying for it
Are you willing to
kill kill kill for it?
to be killed by it?
to disappear utterly
and completely

THE GAMBLER

Your heart has been sterilized, boy
you've had no trials nor tribulations
no challenges to test your grit

the only fire you seem to understand
comes from the oven's pilot light

You can't grasp true glory -
or imagine being trapped in the throes
of an endless summer night

to live without a guarantee
without levels or a scoreboard
no escape

just a high dive -
and the dark valley below

So you've lost your signal huh, boy
and your social media is down

try to imagine a world without wires and wireless
days filled with existential searching
crawling through the muck of your own mind

of not knowing the details of when or why
just the engine of curiosity purring
driving you ever on

of nothing but an ancient ritual
and a rite of passing-through

It's time to put down the tiddlywinks, boy
and pull up a sturdy chair

The devil is handing out his playing cards
and making bittersweet deals

you may want to start praying now
to whatever gods you still know

that you're dealt a royal *lush*
and can still make the horned beast blush

MAY I HAVE THIS DANCE?

All psychedelic freak-outs welcome here
all new and wicked dances begin here
please please bring them to our doorstep

We beg to talk to your strangers
we demand the best of your pushers
we crave the contents of their bags

Share with us your every conceivable high
destroy us with your bottomless lows
shred us to pieces with your never before(s)

Can you stretch our boundaries?
will you please blow our minds?
we sick, numb, and bored
Can you cure us?

sure whatever

this is the momentum of a seeker
the grail of a lost dreamer
a skeleton king on a nightmare throne

ok yeah sure

these are powers that come with a price
pink lipstick upon a terror pig
ignorance is no longer possible

so be it

bring me your best warriors
and let them drink the blood
of all our future wounds

this is man's last chance to transcend
to die and be reborn – pristine and *clean*

CACOPHONY OF SILENCE

The sound of electronic wires
humming compressors and
little red notifications

smothering all
our brain's gamma waves
and heart's frequencies

the flickering screens
dissolving dreams and
plastic visual ice-cream

drowning out
our attempted solutions
and humble evolutions

Signals swarm like thieves
to an unlocked door
stealing our mind's frail grip
upon attention

Our fingers beg to
touch something real
our hearts plead
to be unplugged

There is no wild left
in our wilderness
no transformations remain
in our souls

just a dying battery symbol
and an ever-ticking clock

We're under self-arrest
locked within ourselves
a collapsing prison
of mirrors and reflection

every moment
another cage

DR FRANKENSTEIN UNBOUND

I sit and watch
all these forsaken people
pass me by

Sometimes alone
sometimes in pairs
often in crowds

just wandering around aimless and frantic
untethered from themselves

I can't help but think they're doing it wrong
that what they seek
they already hold
albeit cloaked or thinly veiled

I know there is wealth in a person's solace
an alchemy that transpires from silence
and if the transformation is allowed to complete
it shall provide abundance - not void

We don't need half
of what we're fighting for
damn near dying for

the endless pulsing screens
the winding unconscious streams
the itch within your bones
to be awaken by chaos

By all means -
keep jumping rope with pretty nooses
keep kissing the serpent goodnight
continue to sell your attention for time

We've always been in the eye of a maelstrom
we've always been in the depths of hell
we've always had this burden of choice

but choose once more
choose to know thyself

Discover power in your singularity
reshape years of stale information
into a radiant transition
be the source of the signal

Make it impossible to be lonely
proud to be your own Valentine
make the world your *creation*
become your own Dr. Frankenstein

CARNAL WEAPON

Pink lips pucker
with a shotgun blast

Eyes blink like two
quick and precise guillotines

Lust chokes the air
like poisoned perfume

I have escaped
your fingertips
only to arrive
in the palm
of another hand

I run forever
within your maze
of spiraling circles

death is a *gift*
& Resurrection
is just a state of mind

OLD DOG / NEW TRICK

Snowflakes
like tiny crystal bombs
eyeballs exploding
with every photon

Laughing Spinning Drinking
in the cockpit
a day in the lifetime
of a psychonaut

sprouting wings
and branching out

growing claws
and digging deeper

kicking down doors
and melting through floors

designing new words
and killing old gods

rewiring the motherboard
with a mental broadsword

fucking with the power switch
looking for that perfect glitch

got physics on a dog leash
make that bitch do a new trick

MY NAME IS I DARE

There is an ache
just below the surface

it hides from all
our daily musings

it stalks the borders
of our perception

it softly whispers
its wicked intentions

beneath the cacophony
is where it can be found

feeding off our resistance
twisted and coiled round

on the tip of its demon tongue
lies the answer to every question
you dare to ask

DECAY

The wild weeds bloom
atop our sinking graves
bones held in Earth's tomb

the silver light of the moon
illuminates our past above
out there the beast does croon

new boots arrive to stomp black soil
extinguishing the flames of passion
highways bring the fresh human toil

Observe! the great and vast machine
come to add another thin layer
wipe away our guilt and make us clean

through time and steady decay
we shall build an empire in the dirt
one even the gods could not weigh

~~ANOTHER PARADISE~~

You always made me feel
like a ruler on high
a king in his great castle

standing tall and erect
staring down
into those heavenly eyes

giving me all I have ever desire
and even bit more

such wild energy
flooding into each moment

an overwhelming pleasure
impregnating us with purpose

I imagine even the ancient gods
would have begged to die
in your mouth

RADIATION LOVE SONG

Last night
inside the wet heat of passion
I pulled an insane heart from a deep cavity
and fed it to a Siren's appetite

Beyond all discipline
out of all control
I shed my tired skin and stood naked
under a Chernobyl sky

I became a feast for two starving eyes
my twisted frame was the playground of lust
I rolled down into the dark valley of euphoria
laughing like a madman all the way

I became a child once more
playing with a perfect porcelain doll
in a phosphorene wasteland

My moment there was plumb and fully
engorged like a Halloween candy sack
I was a shattered diamond
rubbed into pulsing crimson skin
I bathed in the beating moonlight
as if it was a fountain of youth

There is no agony to be found
and all my wounds were healed
licked clean and pristine
a nuclear bomb of identity
a gift from a mortal goddess

OPEN SKEYES

All I can hear
is that old
familiar howl

so far away
and yet it calls
from within

it penetrates
my every attempt
to deny

You were wild once
your very breath
mayhem itself

holding life
and death -
all in an instant

unleashed
from the world
you never take prisoners

your eyes are singularities
trapping every moment
within their gaze

you were once free
all your sacred spaces
just extensions of the sky

LOOK AT ME WHEN I'M BURNING ALIVE

Fire Woman
with your
eyes ablaze

you burn your way
to some new paradise

incineration
is your religion
the ashes
are your eternal
disciples

Fire Woman
with your
endless lovers

you smolder your way
South of Eden

revelation
is your favorite game

and in the end
we shall all
worship you

DEMONIC INSURANCE

"Like any good heathen, I'll be there"
I will obey and surely fall
for I belong to you and your siren call

You pull me down into your depths
as deep as they go - so shall I go

my flesh knows no boundaries
my mind roams free and
unattached from the outside world

Your legs spread like vulture's wings
as we scavenge what is left
of this beautiful night

our teeth masticate the sin of our past
our tongues wrap around the dying moment
constricting – we drain the light

because you never really know what you have
until you fuck it and devour it completely

GOURMAND

Have you had enough fat-boy?
of days of love
and nights of lust
of pure indulgence

Have you gorged enough?
on shining moments
strung together like
precious pearls

Can you be satiated?
by this endless feast
of succulent meats and
pristine vegetation

could you stand to go on forever?
could you last 1000 years?
perhaps a million?

gratitude is a capricious animal
that slips from its cage
refusing to be tamed

every morsel of life is a gift
and yet we so easily forget
creatures of habit and void

each day holds raw opportunity
created by every sunrise
destroyed with every sunset

there is a grand victory
in vanquishing your hope
and learning to die *slow*

THE FOOL

Teetering always like a jester
upon the cliff's edge
we mock that we exist at all

Our designer attire
is toxic spit in a wound
already vile and festering

we are drunk dancing monkeys
in a house burning down
all around us

we accelerate the fires
believing ourselves to be
the only creatures of value

weak and unequipped
we never even noticed
the killer in our midst

it creeps closer and closer
whispering words we can no longer
hope to decipher

our frail minds
have turned against themselves
trapped in an ever-closing room

far too powerful
to remain this dumb -
hubris is a potent drug

an incredibly ignorant bet
has been played
in the most dangerous of games

true wisdom seems like
a desert oasis

in an ever-dehydrating world

once we arrived at its shimmering waters
we can never really leave
we drink and become cursed

awakened by the horror of our plight
every drink is just as bitter
as it ever was sweet

PAWN POEM

To hell with the *lazy* King!
and fuck his *spoiled* Queen
she moves without shame
careless for life's game

the Bishops are all cross
with false power
while the Rooks *hide*
behind themselves and cower

the Knights pass *untouched*
by any worthy exchange
but I say - Here, Here
I am here to make a change!

give me a shot at true honor
even though I seem weak and small
for a life without *sacrifice*
is no life at 'all

I know I can never return
moving *forward* until I fall
I was born without purpose
but in death I shall rule them all

WHAT LIES BELOW

Levitating
just above
a glass floor

you can see me
but I couldn't care less

We whirl around
an ever-shifting center
giving birth to feral beasts

becoming the offspring
of some *eldritch* horror
the fate of
every heartbeat

Swimming deeper
than our lungs
can allow

this fresh death
provides
the warmest fire

burn
mystery
burn

your secrets
are as safe
as this night
is long

THANKS ANYWAY

A man with a crucifix
when he really needs a friend

a kid with a loaded gun
but without a proper education

a wise and powerful sage
that never leaves his house

advanced technology
applied only to war

medicine for the sick
behind miles of red tape

rebels who have won
nothing but more chaos

a beautiful woman
forced to hide her face

a pen and a pad
in the hands of the illiterate

a glorious alien world
hidden away in deep space

an elegant song
played for the dead

CUFFED

I've been throwing
fistfuls of silver dollars
into every wishing well
that I discover

I've been pleading
to gin-mad rulers
that just one will land
on the right side of truth

I break every wishbone
that I can find
I even break the ones
not halfway divine

in hopes that someday
somehow
any of this
will matter

every night
I pull from both ends
upon this
American finger-trap

the left is damned
the right is doomed
my hands are always busy
yet they remain entombed

SCULPTOR

don't you dare hold back
pop that vintage bottle
because the only moment
that matters is the present *now*

gush like Mount Tambora
and expel your guts
give'em all you got
and then give a little more

strangle all their doubts
in broad daylight
create destroy repeat
all is bittersweet

prodi-Genius
of abstract romance
idiot savant-eater
in a primordial dance

never leave scraps
devour bones like time
sculpt with your mind
a curious new rhyme

carve and then eat
cut out and swallow
imagination is meat
consume or be hollow

paint with your blood
and waste not a drop
until the canvas is a flood
the art can never stop

GHETTO LOVE

your heart
has become
a ghetto

dark
dangerous
and inadequate

it feeds only
upon itself

your attention
is now a
petty thug

it takes
and takes
but never gives

your love
is hollow and desperate
to survive

yet I keep finding
one more dollar
in my pocket

just to keep
it all alive

ANXIETY

I hear them knocking
at my door
begging for
more more more

I hear them scratching
upon my door
but just as I get up
to see who has arrived
they have all vanished
as if contrived

I hear them pounding
at the door
burrowing beneath
the floor

I hear them banging
all the time
I run to my windows
to try and catch a peek
but they are always gone
without even a squeak

I hear them laughing
their whispers of delight
I hear them even now
those creatures of the night

"Come in! Come in!" I shout
but they make no collision
just flickering ghosts
slipping beyond my vision

FUTILE

They tied
themselves
in such
terrible knots

but every
attempt
to escape

only brought them
closer
together

TEENAGE WASTE LANDER

It never seemed to get
strange enough for me

any attempts to shock me
only put me to sleep
the gore and terror
just got me hard

they were handing out slit wrists
like baseball cards
and I collected them all

I drank all the magic potions
I ate of every poisoned apple
and still I wanted more

the freaks were always my friends
whether I liked it or not
the more fringe their ideas
the more they were attracted to me

I think I saw the death in everything
and because I understood the ending
everything bloomed before my eyes

there was opportunity in excess
a kind of freedom in the extremes
glory in pushing the limits

I demanded it all
I wanted to taste the last drop
disintegrate upon my tongue

there was an evolution in madness
a revelation past the pain
survival of the most fucked

STYX AND STONES

death itself has never been
all that scary to me
it has always seemed a feeble ruler
a one trick pony

suffering on the other hand
is a truly terrifying prospect
a mad king you don't want to piss off
a kind of Renaissance Man of dreadful talents

my imagination runs wild with possibility
the infinite exploitations of organic vessels
the same flesh responsible for pleasure
able to writhe with pain's extremity

or a mind held captive and tortured
stimulated with wires and jolts of electricity
worse yet pulled from the skull and kept alive
but without voice, touch, or vision

No - the thought of *never* dying
is far worse than death could ever be
to feel the sands of time ad infinitum
is what keeps me up at night

this is the true fear of my psyche
not that there is an ending or even expiring
but all the possible doorways
in which one might pass through
to get there

RATED

Hidden catalysts
and spontaneous combustions

skin against skin
tongue around tongue
fangs out

sometimes there's nothing
that can stop love's march

Chemical reactions
and carnal explosions

lust like an emergency
blood racing to the surface
hearts insane with passion

sometimes the best you can do
is hold on for the ride

Maybe it was her long black stockings
squeezing her thighs like a vice grip

maybe it was the slivered moon
tilted in the sky with its coy smirk

maybe it was the stars aligned
casting down their astral temptations

Regardless the reason -
Let love *destroy* you
and don't ask questions

UNTITLED

In the space
between
two breaths
you have
completely
collapsed me

from a
powerful deity
down into
a simple beggar

a kind of
attention slave
not worthy
of his captor

I trade every drop
of my blood
sweat and tears
just to see
you smile

HYDRA

I sever its head
and two more grow in its place
I chop off yet another
and four fill the empty space

I cannot outsmart
this creature of abundance
its power manifests
with growing redundancy

I have given hope
to a hopeless creature
and more reasons
to be my evil teacher

all my swords
are turning within
carving off the edges
of my child's grin

I can no longer ignore
the hydra of self-loathing
it's varied revelations
and all that it's exposing

I must find the strength
to take a mighty swing
one of cauterizing fire
and defeat the devils' plaything

I must sever the fountainhead
leaving nothing, not a trace
and slay the beast I bore
so all my fears can be erased

UNSHACKLED

It is always there just below the surface
waiting to be excavated
its screams of abandonment muffled
by the cacophony in the chambers above

you can feel it relentlessly
pushing and pulsing like a neutron star

it yearns to reach out and touch you
and you yearn back in equal measure
you dream of the buried one
and how she must be released

then all at once like a madman
whose mind has finally snapped
uncontrolled and possessed
you grip the ink pen or the paint brush
as if it was your last breath
and dig your prisoner from his grave

they must breathe once more
they must live again
unrestrained and free
To rage! To rule!
even if it kills *you* in the process

CONTENT

I find it often
in the tranquility
of the morning
but also in the bedlam
of what's to come

I see it always
on the woman's face
as she sleeps
exhausted beside me
from long nights
of raising hell

I sit and take stock
thinking it couldn't be
any other way

It's all been worth it
and I wouldn't
change a thing –
even if I *could*

CALLOUSED

I'm not like them
I don't break
with every Siren call

I wait and they crawl

I choose not to bend
to the whims
of every passing fade

hidden in nightshade

you see - a royal flush
takes true patience
and honest risk

still like a basilisk

their pretty hands
could never hold
these jagged truths

still cosmic youths

their eyes will
never adjust
to something this dark

be your own spark

INSEPARABLE

All the water in the universe
could never wash
your scent from my skin

I could set myself on fire
but it would never
burn you out of me

gravity nor any magnetic force
stands a chance of
pulling you away from me

The sum of all our parts
is far less than
when we are together

NEW MOON

Her hands were like
hungry vultures
that pulled meat
from my desperate body

her eyes were like
shallow pools
as dark as new moons
begging to not exist at all

her mouth was
my judge, jury, and executioner
lips like two guillotines
and yet I could never resist

with every kiss a
a bitter surrender
with every blowjob
my heart in a blender

FADING LIGHT

Don't just stand there Old Man!
kiss the beautiful woman
take her by the hand
and dive into the unknown

life is far too short
to squander these opportunities
to pass on your chances

don't ignore the good vibes
the guts don't lie
you got lucky
but it still *counts*
so, kiss the goddess
before you turn to stone

she flows with ancient power
glows with a sacred mystery
she is the answer
to an unasked question

don't choke Old Man!
kiss her before the sun appears
and you no longer can

TOMB WITH A VIEW

When any given night
becomes "the great escape"
no need for planes or trains

when the bedroom
becomes a tropical oasis
from the outside world

when you no longer
give a single fuck
about what anyone thinks at all

when you never need to leave
and are always arriving
that's when you know
you've won the game

STARVING NIGHT

I can't help
but tear your clothes
from your aching bones

throw you down
upon this haunted bed
and empty my fool's head

I can't stop
what has begun
and seems to have no end

there are no exits
for this kind of hell
only exhaustion and a death knell

we make the demon with
an infinite back
and say our hollow prayers

I crawl forever
toward your starving night
never getting anywhere

THE STALKER

My cravings come alive
beneath the moon
and it's quicksilver light

like some nocturnal creature
that slinks and slithers
its path hidden by night

Her eyes sink
like a southern crocodile
in some endless abyss

and down in that empty plane
we feed and feed until
our bodies get their bliss

A ritual has begun
and now death joins
passion and love in the moment

we are unnatural born killers
killing what is left of
of each and every second

MEDITATION ON THE BLESSING OF DEATH

When death comes knocking at my door
it will be unlocked
and I will say, "Come in, Come right in!"

I don't intend to be rude
and leave her waiting

because the scariest thing I can imagine
is a product of immortality
an actual endless existence
a forever being - ad infinitum

just think of all the possible circumstances
one could find themselves in
if given the blessing/curse of never ending

eternal imprisonment
unabashed torture
Dorian Gray level ennui

how can anything mean anything at all?
if it is no longer rare
nor hard to obtain

just because your body is alive
does not signify all its potential conditions

try and wrap your mind around
all the varieties of human pain and delusion
or worse yet the possibility
of some future enslaver

some-kind of alien-sadist
who has the ability to exploit
every nuance of our biochemical systems

the tools of infinite malice
gripped in the skilled hands
of a celestial destroyer

No, save your immortality
hold back your eternal life
I want my death served on time
whatever time that might be

I want no permanence
no cyclical resurrection
no ritual last supper
the ephemeral ones I've had
are sufficient enough

I want exactly what I've got
and nothing more

so all I've had and may still come
remains pure and imperfect
the proverbial rose that blooms
then fades and finally dies
like all great things

death is a greedy lover
but to deny her
is cosmic horror indeed

SUGAR AND SALT

Pale heavens flicker and die out
as the mortal garden flowers
burst into full bloom

the days decay and threaten
to slip away
the nights evolve and demand
their ferryman's pay

bliss left untasted
is worth nothing at all
euphoria is a delicate dance
but ends in an angel's fall

breathe in exotic perfume
and taste the forbidden fruits

let love's poison creep
deep into your bones

linger and wallow
in every drop of passion's blood

align your sorrows
with oblivion's sword

scatter all despair
into the endless sky

push past death's flimsy gate
and dive heart first
into the salt of life

COMMENTARY ON MEMORY AND CHOICE

fragmented and degraded
shattered and partitioned
eroded by sensory storms
worn away by the years

the sands of time are so abrasive
to the neuronal film within our skulls

did you remember not to forget?
did you lock up all your precious moments?
did you leave the lights on?
we all fall asleep
at the wheel of fortune - eventually

the "good times" flickering
like failing Halloween lights
in ever darkening alleys of our mind

your first kiss now just fading imagery
the memory like a junkie
begging for a hit just to stay alive
the tears, the laughter, the pain
the details but a whisper
to a once booming choir

can you recall much of it at all?
even a fraction of the sprawl?
will you feed the memories most in need?
it's just the gods playing dice when they're bored
changing the channel on the human race

in the meantime - bring me supreme intoxication
serve me my sacred absentia
and blessed amnesia

for I cannot bear the thought
that you have forgotten
the universe between our lips

SLAYER & SLAVED

When fate
finally arrives
to pull the trigger
to drop the guillotine
to hand out the aneurysm

I'll be there

dressed in the flames
of own self-destruction
bearing the weight
of a shattered crown

When fate
comes a knockin'
with a bittersweet kiss
with poisoned apple
with a drink and a match

I'll be there

to burn like a slow candle
in Hell's furnace
waiting to be sure
the transformation is complete

There are a thousand ways
to die a slave
but only one way to become
your own master

PUNCTURED

As I walked along the southern California coast at four in the morning
I thought I heard a maddening crowd
somewhere off in the pale moonlight
but after many a paranoid gander
my eyes perceived no one to account for my palpable hallucination

There was nothing on that cold wet sand but me
a few tiny translucent hermit crabs
and countless ocean waves crashing to my side

As I advanced along the shoreline my illusion
began to grow and take shape
I once again heard the strange and vibrant crowd
but this time a fully formed vision was soon to follow

I caught a punctuated glimpse into some far off timescape
unsure if it was from the distant past
somehow pushing forward and finding my consciousness
or if it was from a hypothetical future calling back
perhaps a touch of both - meeting somewhere in the *middle*

The tides seemed to whisper to me through it all
of some vital intention or maybe a stern warning
within its constant swell came a cacophony
of mystic voices and ethereal sounds

The penetrating murmurs amplified into a wall of command
a direct order for me to submit
an inescapable surrendering was upon me
to deny its power was lunacy
to ignore its wealth reeked of spiritual suicide

The Pacific Ocean had opened its terrible and beautiful maw
finding me like a failed hero as ancient gods do
it lapped its endless tongue upon the edges of my mind
it seemed as if it had always been there –
waiting for me to arrive in that precise moment
waiting to pounce like some coy cosmic cat
ready to swallow me whole
and then in an instant it all vanished
replaced with a quiet and haunting laughter

From that moment until now
I will never forget (nor could I)
what it means
to touch the sublime

ENDANGERED

there's a fire in the cockpit
and a vulture in our waiting room
our love has become
an endangered species

Evolution Revolution
we're chasing our tails

there is a fire in the cockpit
vultures gathering in our waiting room
We've got to get out!

Devolution No Absolution
it's just the snake eating his tail

because we're dying, we're dying
we're all dead and reborn

there's a fire in the cockpit
a flood of vultures in the waiting room
our love has become

an endangered species
or subspecies
a whole new species

Evolution No Solution
we are the beautiful and *damned*

because we're dying, we're dying
we're all dead and reborn

There's a fire in the cockpit
and starving vultures pouring through the gate
our love has become
the most dangerous of species
We've got to get out!

LITANY

dissolve your excuses
destroy all exits
implode entirely
and then explode completely

recreate matter
burn all results
reinvent yourself
on the torture rack & wheel

demolish stale fates
make life a slave
choose to endure
risk it all on the unluckiest horse

shed some skin
wear out the bit
drive over the edge
swallow her like a galaxy

chew away the points
eat the forbidden fruit
flood the mind's eye
drown the masters in their sleep

play dice with God
make love in the devil's bedroom
worship nothing
and devour everything

IMAGO

In every drop of my blood
spilled and spent
was a birth of opportunity
a crimson river
leading to the hard truth

In every salty tear
ripped from my skull
was a healing catharsis
the shedding of a
useless skin

Pain is proportional
to progress
a life well lived
will always demand
its payment -
the dark ferryman
his two gold coins

No matter how sharp
the blades of circumstance
No matter the scars
of sacrifice
the trick is to enjoy
the process

Beauty is always balanced
by its beasts
love was never innocent
only ignorant
to its power

*The dance with death
was the only thing
keeping me alive*

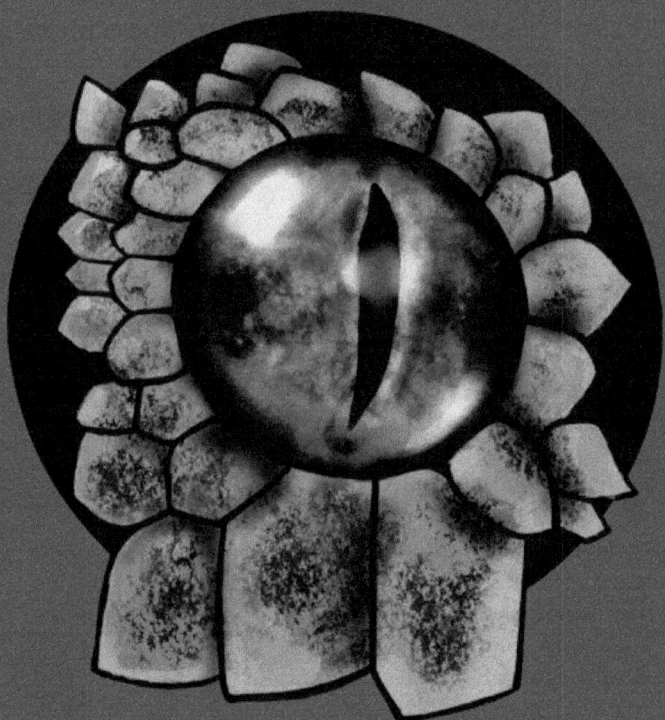

Ryan Morrow is an analytical chemist and poet living in Minneapolis, Minnesota. In his free time from the laboratory he writes poetry about his experiences and observations of the world. His style is a chimera of the idealized writers of old and a more modern free verse. His poems span the gamut of topic and form, but are always pushing boundaries with curious and demanding intent.

To date he has released three volumes. "Chase Something Worth the Kill," his literary cherry-pop from 2015 that has been reimagined and reworked here. It's pages are filled with punchy lines of verse that often leave the reader captivated and perplexed all at once. After that came the hefty and exploratory "Deep Survival" of 2018. A more focused effort on the dualities of being. Finally in 2020, Mr. Morrow released his third and most ambitious work, "Weightless." A book about beauty and its beasts, the ephemeral nature of man, and falling in love with uncertainty.

It's safe to say that Ryan has not yet exhausted himself of the written word. Much more territory lays waiting to be explored and brought to the surface. Sit back and enjoy the ride.

www.ingramcontent.com/pod-product-compliance
Lightning Source LLC
Chambersburg PA
CBHW071858090426
42811CB00004B/661